Duet Classics
•for Piano•

Book 2

Selected and Edited by Gayle Kowalchyk and E. L. Lancaster

ABOUT THIS COLLECTION

The first known keyboard duets were written as early as the late 16th or early 17th century. Since that time, many composers have written original works for the medium.

This collection contains 16 duets in their original form written by 9 composers who lived in the 18th, 19th and 20th centuries. To facilitate reading for younger students, the primo and secondo parts are on separate pages. Each duet has been carefully edited and fingered for ease in performance by intermediate students. Both parts contain measure numbers for easy reference.

These duets can be used as supplementary material for any course of study. They are excellent repertoire selections for group lessons, ensemble classes or "monster" concerts. Students will be motivated by music-making with friends as they acquire security with tempo and rhythm provided by ensemble performance. Enjoy!

Cover design: Greg McKinney
Art direction: Ted Engelbart

SECONDO

March
from *The Children's Musical Friend*

Heinrich Wohlfahrt (1797–1883)
Op. 87, No. 44

Moderato

PRIMO

March
from *The Children's Musical Friend*

Heinrich Wohlfahrt (1797–1883)
Op. 87, No. 44

SECONDO

Galop
from *The Children's Musical Friend*

Heinrich Wohlfahrt (1797–1883)
Op. 87, No. 46

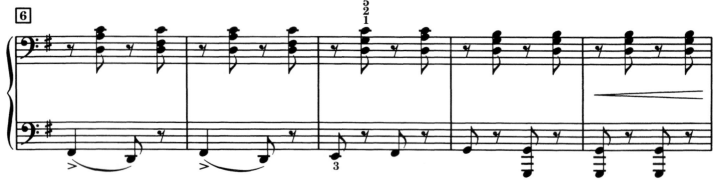

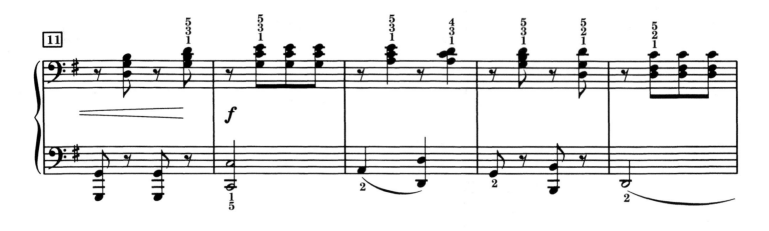

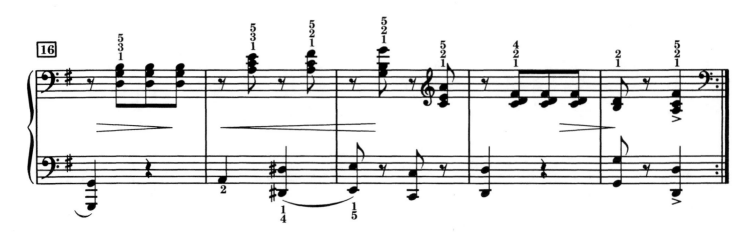

PRIMO

Galop
from *The Children's Musical Friend*

Heinrich Wohlfahrt (1797–1883)
Op. 87, No. 46

6

SECONDO

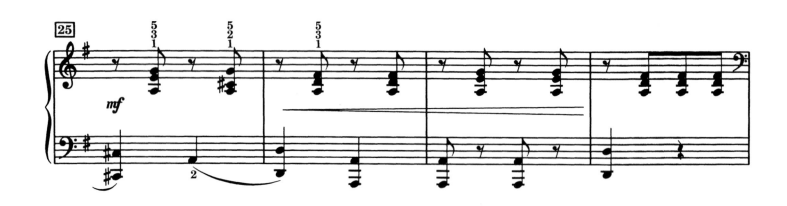

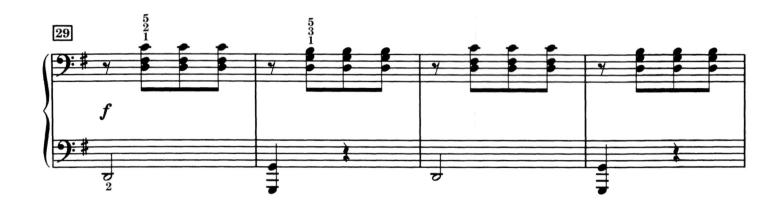

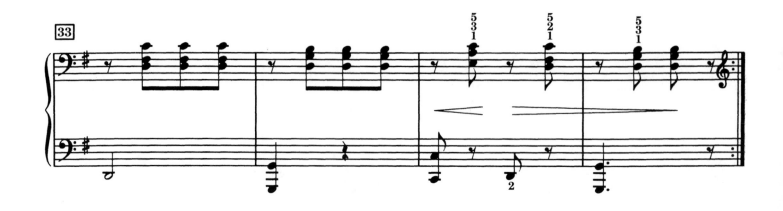

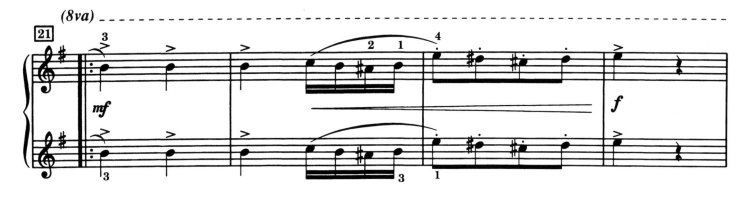

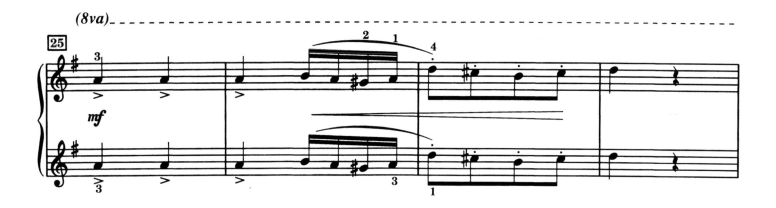

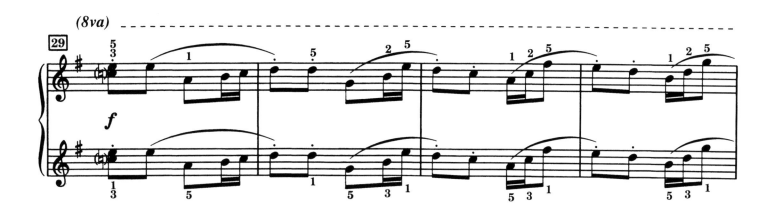

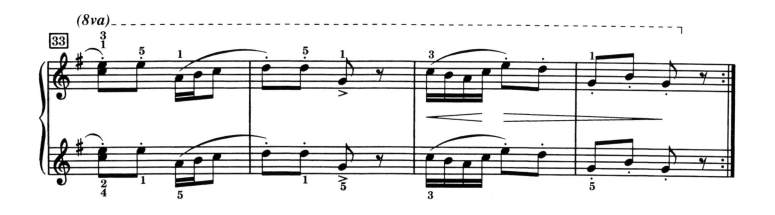

Rondino

from *Melodious Pieces*

Anton Diabelli (1781–1858)
Op. 149, No. 17

PRIMO

Rondino
from *Melodious Pieces*

Anton Diabelli (1781–1858)
Op. 149, No. 17

SECONDO

Allegro in E Minor
from *Melodious Pieces*

Anton Diabelli (1781–1858)
Op. 149, No. 28

PRIMO

Allegro in E Minor
from *Melodious Pieces*

Anton Diabelli (1781–1858)
Op. 149, No. 28

Waltz

Alexander Gretchaninoff (1864–1956)
Op. 98, No. 15

Tempo di Valse

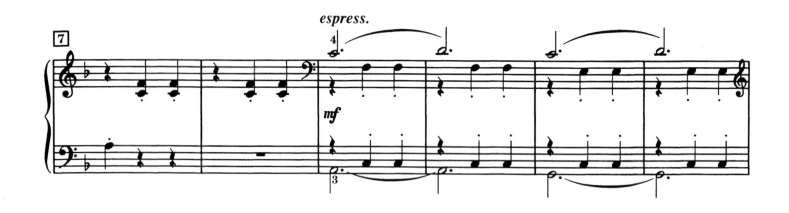

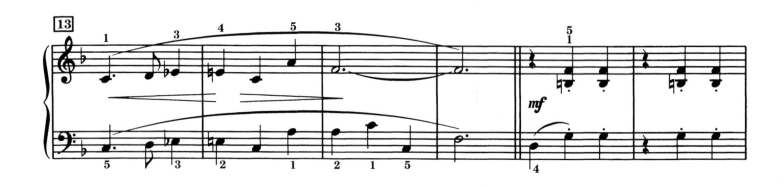

PRIMO

Waltz

Alexander Gretchaninoff (1864–1956)
Op. 98, No. 15

Tempo di Valse

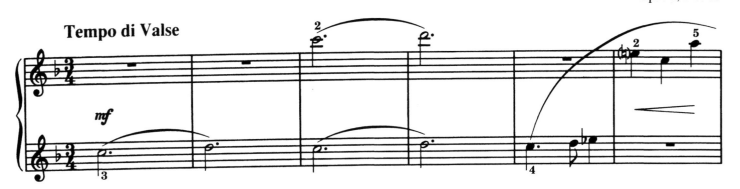

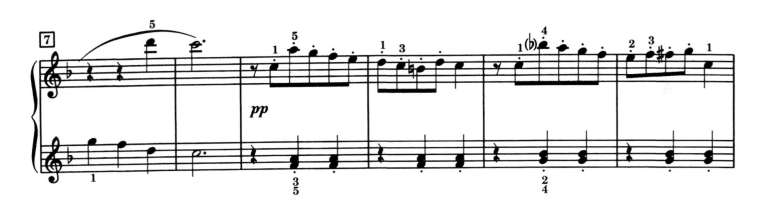

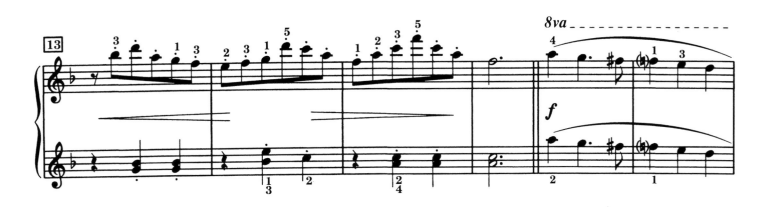

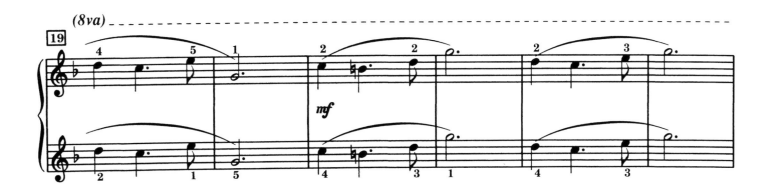

14

SECONDO

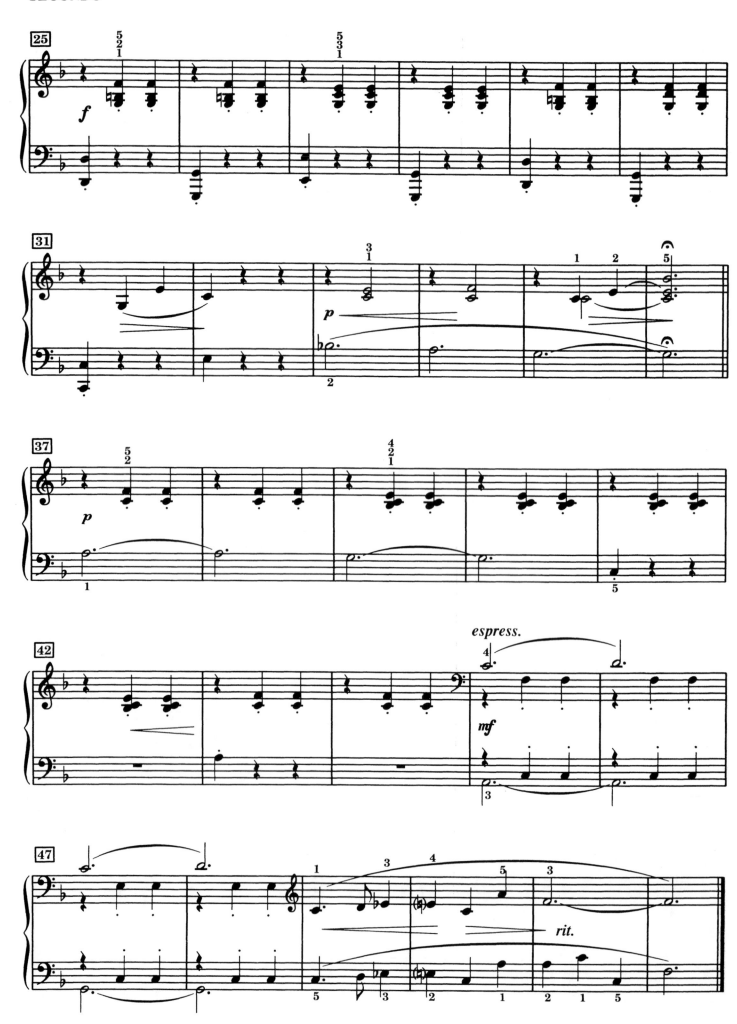

PRIMO

Three Little Pieces
II.

Anton Bruckner
(1824–1896)

Allegro moderato

PRIMO

Three Little Pieces

II.

Anton Bruckner
(1824–1896)

SECONDO

Three Little Pieces
III.

Anton Bruckner
(1824–1896)

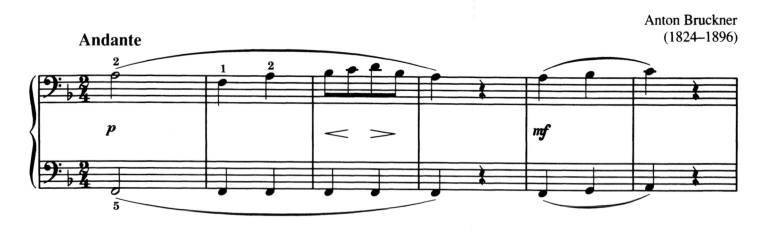

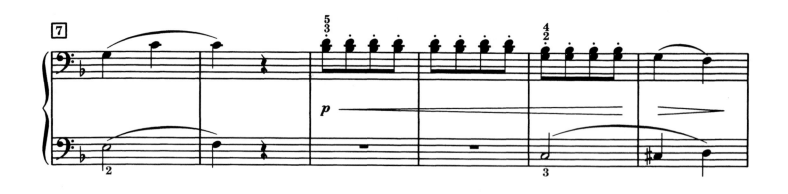

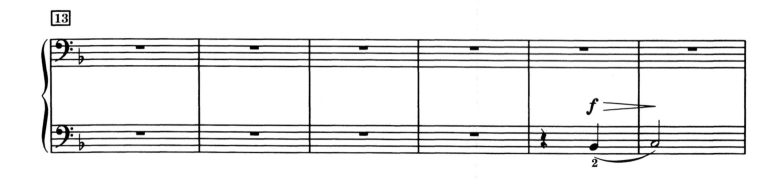

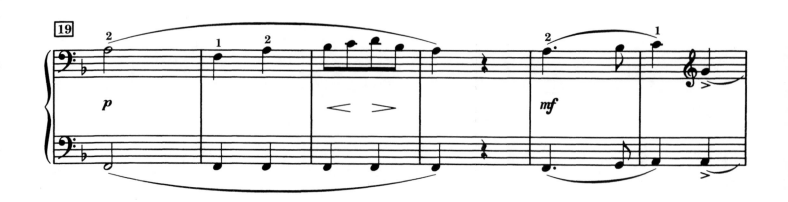

PRIMO

Three Little Pieces
III.

Anton Bruckner
(1824–1896)

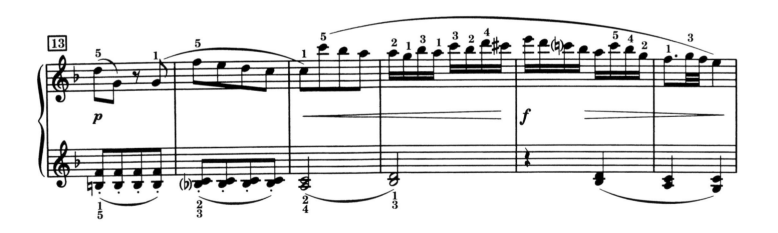

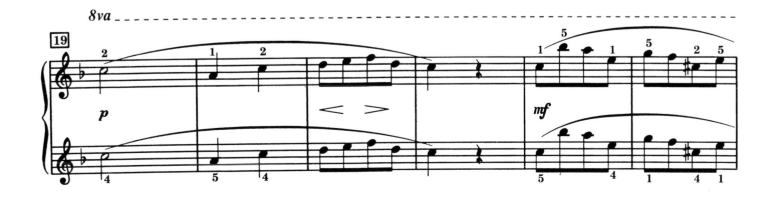

SECONDO

PRIMO

SECONDO

Venetian Gondolier's Song

Oskar Fried (1871–1941)
Op. 6, No. 3

PRIMO

Venetian Gondolier's Song

Oskar Fried (1871–1941)
Op. 6, No. 3

SECONDO

Sonatina in G Major

Anton André (1775–1842)
Op. 45, No. 2

PRIMO

Sonatina in G Major

Anton André (1775–1842)
Op. 45, No. 2

Rondo

Allegretto

PRIMO

Rondo

Allegretto

SECONDO

Andante
from *Five Easy Pieces*

Igor Stravinsky
(1882–1971)

PRIMO

Andante
from *Five Easy Pieces*

Igor Stravinsky
(1882–1971)

SECONDO

Balalaika
from *Five Easy Pieces*

Igor Stravinsky
(1882–1971)

Balalaika

from *Five Easy Pieces*

PRIMO

Igor Stravinsky
(1882–1971)

SECONDO

PRIMO

Andantino
from *Pleasures of Youth*

Anton Diabelli (1781–1858)
Op. 163, No. 2

Andantino cantabile

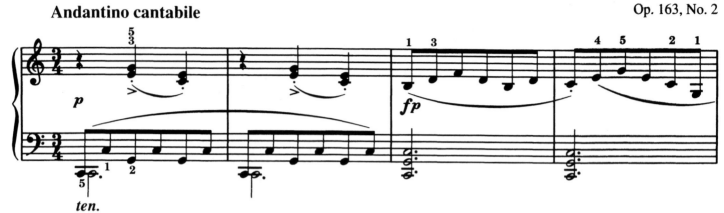

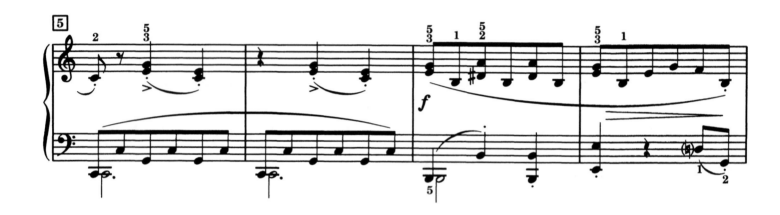

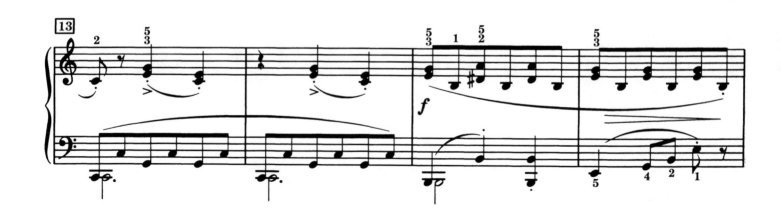

PRIMO

Andantino
from *Pleasures of Youth*

Anton Diabelli (1781–1858)
Op. 163, No. 2

Andantino cantabile

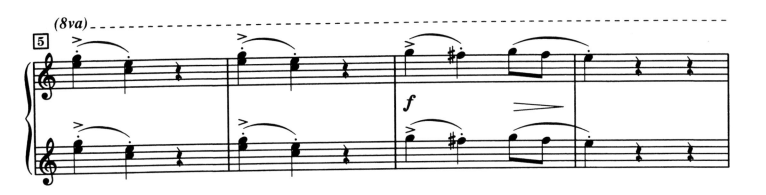

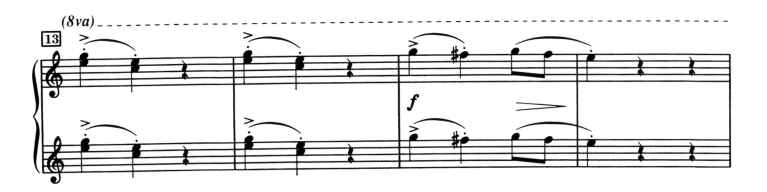

SECONDO

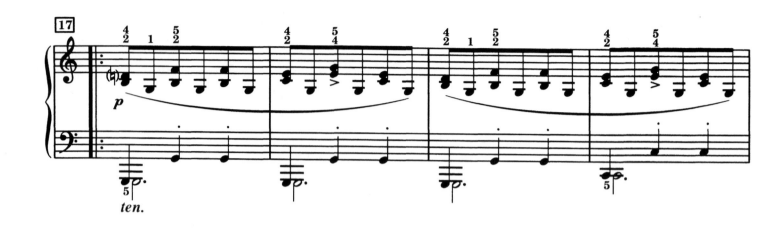

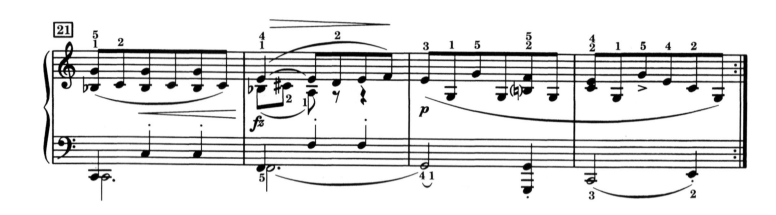

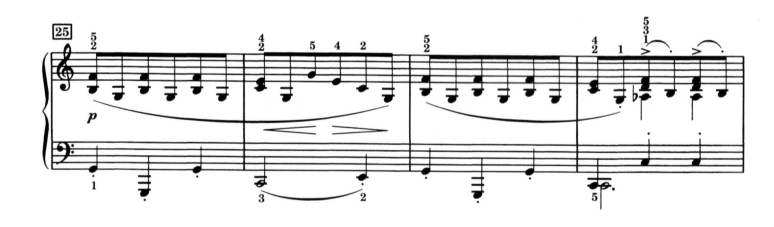

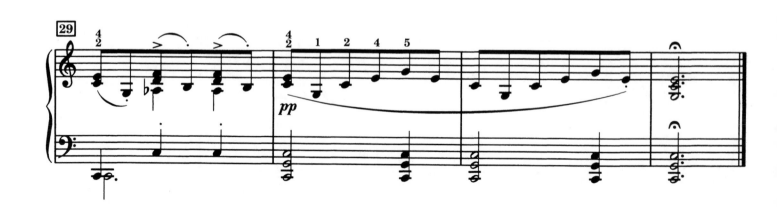

PRIMO

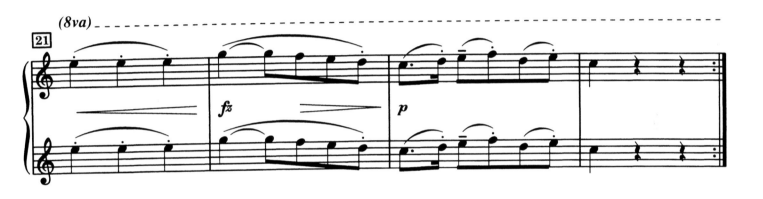

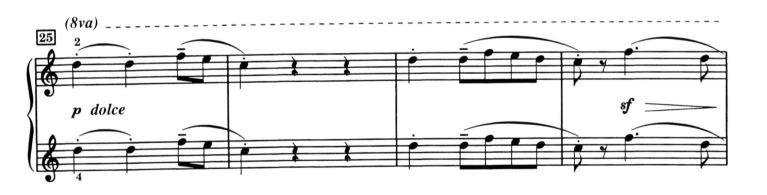

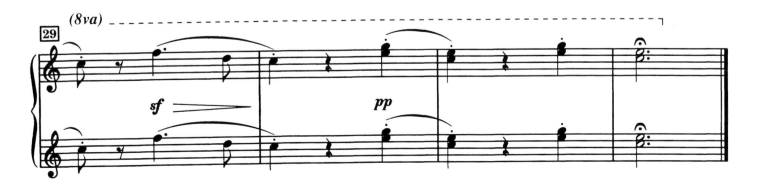

SECONDO

Rondo
from *Pleasures of Youth*

Anton Diabelli (1781–1858)
Op. 163, No. 2

Allegro moderato

Rondo
from *Pleasures of Youth*

Anton Diabelli (1781–1858)
Op. 163, No. 2

PRIMO

Allegro moderato

SECONDO

PRIMO

SECONDO

Barcarolle

Zdeněk Fibich (1850–1900)
Op. 22, No. 2

PRIMO

Barcarolle

Zdeněk Fibich (1850-1900)
Op. 22, No. 2

SECONDO

Shepherd's Poem

Franz Bendel (1833–1874)
Op. 43, No. 3

PRIMO

Shepherd's Poem

Franz Bendel (1833–1874)
Op. 43, No. 3

SECONDO

PRIMO

About the Composers

Anton André (1775–1842) was a German pianist, violinist, composer and publisher. His book on harmony and counterpoint was highly respected during his lifetime. In 1841, he published the thematic catalog that Mozart had kept of his own works.

Franz Bendel (1833–1874), a German pianist and composer, studied in Prague with Proksch and in Weimar with Liszt. He later taught at Kullak's Academy in Berlin. His works for piano include a piano concerto, a piano trio and several salon pieces.

Anton Bruckner (1824–1896), an Austrian, is best known as an orchestral composer. He taught both theory and organ at the Conservatory in Vienna. The selections in this collection are the second and third of three small duets that he composed.

Anton Diabelli (1781–1858), an Austrian publisher and composer, wrote numerous piano duets. He was the publisher of Schubert's first printed works. An experienced musician, piano teacher and composer, he was able to respond to musical trends of the day. Consequently, his publishing company was a huge financial success.

Zdeněk Fibich (1850–1900) was a significant Czech composer. He first studied in Prague and then at the Leipzig Conservatory. Upon returning to Prague, he occupied several important posts as a choral conductor. He composed operas, orchestral works and wrote a piano method.

Oskar Fried (1871–1941), a German, was a conductor and composer. He studied in Frankfurt and Berlin and played the horn in various orchestras. He held numerous positions as a conductor in Germany prior to 1934 when he went to Russia. He continued his conducting career in that country and became a Soviet citizen in 1940.

Alexander Gretchaninoff (1864–1956), a Russian, studied at the Moscow Conservatory with Arensky and at the St. Petersburg Conservatory with Rimsky-Korsakov. He settled in New York in 1939 and became a United States citizen in 1946.

Igor Stravinsky (1882–1971), a Russian composer, had a profound influence on the evolution of music in the 20th century. A prolific composer, he wrote works for the stage, orchestra, chamber music, vocal music and piano music. He became an American citizen in 1945 and the U.S. Postal Service issued a 2¢ stamp bearing his image in 1982.

Heinrich Wohlfahrt (1797–1883) was a German composer and piano teacher. He wrote a large quantity of educational piano music, including original music and arrangements. The selections in this collection are from *The Children's Musical Friend*, which contains 50 duets in progressive order.